# Apple Vision Pro User Guide

## Unlocking the Full Potential of Your Revolutionary Spatial Computing Device

**Alfred A Weeks**

# Table of contents

# Chapter 1. Introduction

## Overview of Apple Vision Pro

Apple Vision Pro is a spatial computer that allows you to navigate with your eyes, hands, and voice while integrating digital content and apps into your physical environment. An extensive overview of the device, including instructions on how to set it up, customize the fit, and use simple gestures, can be found in the Apple Vision Pro User Guide. The tutorial also explains how to use iCloud, link Bluetooth devices, connect to the internet, and log in with your Apple ID. Notes, Photos, Messages, and Safari are among the built-in apps on Apple Vision Pro. You can open these apps in Home View by simply tapping on them, or you can ask Siri to do so. You can find compatible iPad and iPhone apps in the App Store on Apple Vision Pro, along with games and apps made specifically for your device. Creating the workspace of your dreams, playing your favorite games from the Apple Arcade and App Store, watching your favorite shows and movies in the Cinema Environment in the Apple TV app, and even having an up-close and personal encounter with dinosaurs in a brand-new interactive experience are just a few of the advantages of utilizing Apple Vision Pro. Learn how to protect your Apple ID using the privacy and security features already included in the guide. If you want to make the most of your Apple Vision Pro, this guide is a great resource.

## Benefits of using Apple Vision Pro

With its many advantages, the Apple Vision Pro is a ground-breaking spatial computer. Some of the main advantages include:

**Immersive Experiences:** To create really immersive augmented reality experiences, the Vision Pro can project 3D items into your existing surroundings or carry you to other locations.

**Seamless Integration:** The gadget makes it possible for natural and immersive interactions with the virtual world by smoothly integrating digital material into your real area.

**Sophisticated Sensors and Processing Power:** For precise object placement and accurate depth perception, the Vision Pro is equipped with a set of sophisticated sensors, including LiDAR. The Apple silicon processor is specially crafted to deliver exceptional performance for AR and AI applications.

**Connection and spatial audio:** The Vision Pro provides smooth communication with other devices thanks to its Wi-Fi, Bluetooth, and cellular connection. Additionally, it provides spatial audio technology for a three-dimensional audio experience.

**Development Tools and APIs:** The Vision Pro provides high-level APIs, such as motion tracking, scene interpretation, and light estimation, to developers so they may create augmented reality experiences. Additionally, it offers an extensive collection of APIs and development tools to facilitate the development of innovative augmented reality apps.

These features set the Apple Vision Pro apart as a cutting-edge tool that unites the digital and physical domains to create a whole new range of possibilities.

## How to use this guide

To ensure optimal utilization of the Apple Vision Pro User Guide, adhere to the following steps:

**1. Get acquainted with the device:** Recognise the fundamental characteristics and operations of the Apple Vision Pro, such as its spatial computing powers and the methods by which you may use your hands, eyes, and voice to interact with it.

**2. Navigation and Interaction:** Get acquainted with the many gestures and voice commands that you may use to operate the Apple Vision Pro by learning how to navigate VisionOS, the operating system.

**3. Connectivity and Multimedia:** Learn how to utilize iCloud, connect Bluetooth devices, connect the Apple Vision Pro to the internet, and login in with your Apple ID. Learn about the device's multimedia features, such as how to see and use spatial photographs and videos, make FaceTime conversations, and access entertainment material.

**4. Customization and Security:** Learn how to personalize your use of the Apple Vision Pro by configuring its display settings, securing your Apple ID with built-in privacy and security features, and setting it up for work.

**Developer Resources:** The book details the development tools and APIs available for the Apple Vision Pro, which developers can use to create augmented reality experiences. These APIs include high-level ones for motion tracking, scene interpretation, and light estimates.

# Chapter 2. Getting Started

## Setting up Apple Vision Pro

Unpacking, adjusting the fit, and turning on the device are the simple steps involved in setting up the Apple Vision Pro. Here's a thorough guide:

**1. Unboxing**: Gently take the Apple Vision Pro out of its package, making sure that the headset, charging cord, and power adapter are all included.

**2. Adjusting the Fit**: To guarantee a snug and comfortable fit, the Apple Vision Pro has dials and straps that can be adjusted. Use the dial to fine-tune the fit and adjust the straps to suit your head.

**3. Turning on the headset:** Press and hold the power button until the Apple logo displays. To finish the initial setup, connect to Wi-Fi and sign in with your Apple ID by following the on-screen prompts.

**4. Basic Navigation:** After the device is configured, get acquainted with the hand gestures, voice commands, and eye tracking features of basic navigation. To learn how to utilize these capabilities in detail, go to the Apple Vision Pro User Guide.

**5. Connectivity and Multimedia:** Establish an internet connection, log in using your Apple ID, and investigate the multimedia features of the Apple Vision Pro. These include FaceTime chats, watching 3D images and movies, and accessing entertainment content.

**6. Customization and Security:** Utilize the Apple Vision Pro's built-in privacy and security features to safeguard your Apple ID, as well as display settings and work-related configurations.

You can easily set up and start using the Apple Vision Pro by following these instructions.

## Basic gestures and controls

Users may effortlessly engage with the Apple Vision Pro thanks to its range of simple motions and controls. The following provides a thorough summary of the fundamental motions and controls:

### Hand Gestures:
- *Tap:* Just as on an iPhone, tapping the thumb and index finger together tells the headset that you want to touch a virtual element on the screen.

- *Double Tap*: The double tap gesture is started by tapping twice.

*- Pinch and Hold:* This motion is used to highlight text and is comparable to the tap and hold gesture.

*- Pinch and Drag:* This function allows you to scroll and reposition windows. The speed at which users move their hands determines the scrolling pace, whether vertically or horizontally.

*- Zoom:* To zoom in or out, users may press their fingers together and draw their hands apart, respectively. You can also change the window's size by dragging its corners.

*- Rotate*: To control virtual objects, do this two-handed motion by squeezing your fingers together and rotating your hands.

## Eye Gestures:

The several cameras in the Vision Pro monitor the user's gaze with remarkable precision. Eye gestures and hand movements coordinate with one another. When employing hand gestures to target what the user wishes to engage with, eye location is crucial.

## Digital Crown and Top Button:

The Digital Crown and top button may be used to launch Home View, recenter content into the user's field of vision, change the volume or immersion, transition between the outside world and digital material, and take pictures.

## Voice Input:

Users may communicate with the Apple Vision Pro by speaking aloud in addition to using gestures.

Users may explore and interact with the Apple Vision Pro in a natural and immersive manner thanks to the combination of these gestures and controls.

# Capturing images and videos

You can use the following procedures to capture pictures and films with the Apple Vision Pro:

## Capture spatial images and videos:

- To activate capture, press the top button.

- Select whether you want to take a picture or a movie in space, then hit the top button to begin taking a picture or a video in space.

- Press the top button one more time or touch to end the recording.

## Best Practices for Capturing:

- When capturing spatial video, try to maintain head motionlessness. When you capture spatial video, a crosshair appears in the middle of your field of vision. If you move too much, the crosshair looks like it's outside of a circle. For the best viewing pleasure, keep the crosshair within the circle.

- If you tilt your head, a level is shown via the shutter button before beginning a recording. This might serve as a guide to help you take more level shots and films.

- Steer clear of taking pictures or films of people who are quite near you.

**View and Share:**

- Launch the Photos app and choose "Spatial" from the tab bar to see your spatial images and movies.

- Open Photos, locate the image or video you want to share, hit the share button, and choose an option like AirDrop, Mail, or Messages to share a spatial capture.

## Extra Options:

- You may also use the voice command "Siri, take a screenshot," or you can press the Digital Crown and the top button at the same time to snap a still picture of your view.

- Open Control Center, press the record button, and then end the recording when you're done to capture your view.

These instructions make it simple to use the Apple Vision Pro to take and share spatial images and movies.

# Chapter 3. Product Features

## Overview of Apple Vision Pro features

With its many cutting-edge capabilities, the Apple Vision Pro is a revolutionary spatial computer that will improve your digital experiences. Here is a thorough rundown of the salient characteristics:

1. **Spatial Computing:** By smoothly integrating digital material into your physical environment, the Apple Vision Pro creates immersive augmented reality experiences.

2. **Modern Sensors and Processing Power:** For precise item placement and accurate depth perception, the gadget is equipped with a suite of modern sensors, including LiDAR. The Apple silicon processor

is specially crafted to deliver exceptional performance for AR and AI applications.

**3. Connection and Spatial Audio:** The Apple Vision Pro can communicate with other devices wirelessly thanks to its Wi-Fi, Bluetooth, and cellular connection. Additionally, it provides spatial audio technology for a three-dimensional audio experience.

**4. Development Tools and APIs:** The Apple Vision Pro provides high-level APIs, including motion tracking, scene interpretation, and light estimation, allowing developers to create augmented reality experiences. Additionally, it offers an extensive collection of APIs and development tools to facilitate the development of innovative augmented reality apps.

**5. Built-in applications:** The Apple Vision Pro has a number of built-in applications, including Notes, Photos, Messages, and Safari. You may ask Siri to launch an app from Home View, or you can touch it to open it.

**6. App Store:** Compatible iPad and iPhone applications, as well as games made specifically for your device, may be found in the App Store on Apple Vision Pro.

**7. Customization and Security:** Utilize the Apple Vision Pro's built-in privacy and security features to safeguard your Apple ID, as well as customize your experience by configuring the device for work and changing the display settings.

**8. Basic movements and controls:** Users can effortlessly interact with the Apple Vision Pro thanks to its simple movements and controls.

**9. Taking Pictures and Videos:** Use the Photos app to quickly and easily take and share spatial pictures and videos with others.

Knowing these features allows you to get the most out of Apple Vision Pro.

## Using visionOS apps

The VisionOS operating system on the Apple Vision Pro comes with a number of integrated apps and features that are meant to improve your digital experiences. This is a thorough rundown of how to use VisionOS apps:

**1. Built-in Apps:** Notes, Photos, Messages, and Safari are among the built-in apps on the Apple Vision Pro. You can launch these apps in Home View by simply tapping them, or you can ask Siri to do so.

**2. App Store:** You can find compatible iPad and iPhone apps here, along with games and apps made specifically for your device, in the App Store on Apple Vision Pro.

**3. Home View:** Your apps and features are accessible through Home View, which serves as your main hub. Simply tap to open your apps from Home View, or ask Siri to do so.

**4. Siri:** If you need help navigating and interacting with your Apple Vision Pro, Siri is a strong assistant. Siri allows you to manage your device, launch apps, and do information searches.

**5. Notes:** Organize your thoughts, make checklists, and take notes with the Notes app. To write and draw on your notes, you can also use the Apple Pencil.

**6. Photos:** With the Photos app, you can open, alter, and distribute your images and videos. With the Apple Vision Pro, you can also produce 3D images and videos.

**7. Messages:** Use the Messages app to send and receive messages, make FaceTime calls, and share content.

**8. Safari:** To browse the internet, use the Safari app. You can use the Apple Pencil to write and draw on webpages.

**9. Apple Music:** Download and use the Apple Music app.

**10. Apple TV:** In the Cinema Environment, use the Apple TV app to watch your favorite movies and television shows.

**11.** Play your favorite games from the App Store and **Apple Arcade**.

**12.** Use the **Apple Fitness** app to stay active and healthy.

By understanding these VisionOS apps, you can make the most of your Apple Vision Pro experience.

## Connecting to the internet

Use these procedures to get the Apple Vision Pro online:

**1. To turn on Apple Vision Pro**, press and hold the power button until the Apple logo displays to turn on the Apple Vision Pro.

**2. Configure Wi-Fi:** To connect to your Wi-Fi network during the initial setup phase, follow the on-screen directions. Go to Settings > Wi-Fi and choose the network you want to connect to if you need to establish a fresh connection.

**3. Enter a Wi-Fi password:** If the Wi-Fi network asks for a password, use the Apple Pencil or the on-screen keyboard.

**4. Verify internet connection:** After connecting, open the Settings app and select Wi-Fi to confirm your internet connection. If a checkbox appears next to your Wi-Fi network, you are connected to the internet.

**5. Connect to a cellular network:** If your Apple Vision Pro is capable of supporting cellular connections, you may do so by navigating to Settings > Cellular and choosing the desired cellular plan.

**6. Check cellular connection:** After connecting, open the Settings app and choose Cellular to check your cellular connection. If your plan has a checkbox next to it, you are connected to the cellular network.

You may have a flawless digital experience by connecting the Apple Vision Pro to the internet and following these instructions.

## Signing in with your Apple ID

To log in to the Apple Vision Pro using your Apple ID, do the following actions:

**1. To turn on Apple Vision Pro**, press and hold the power button until the Apple logo displays to turn on the Apple Vision Pro.

**2. Configure Wi-Fi:** To connect to your Wi-Fi network during the initial setup phase, follow the on-screen directions.

**3. Enter your Apple ID and password:** You may use the Apple Pencil or the on-screen keyboard to enter your Apple ID and password during the first setup procedure.

**4. Activating two-factor authentication** for your Apple ID may require entering a verification code sent to your phone number or trusted device.

**5. Use Touch ID or Face ID to log in:** If your Apple Vision Pro is compatible, you may use Touch ID or Face ID to log in rather than typing your Apple ID and password.

**6. Verify Apple ID:** After logging in, go to Settings > Your Name to see your Apple ID.

**7. Sign out:** Go to Settings, then select Your Name. Sign out to log out of your Apple ID.

You may have a smooth digital experience on the Apple Vision Pro by following these steps to sign in with your Apple ID.

**Note:** You may find troubleshooting procedures on the Apple Support page if you run into any problems while logging in with your Apple ID.

## Using iCloud on Apple Vision Pro

To use iCloud on the Apple Vision Pro, do the following actions:

**1.** To **turn on Apple Vision Pro**, press and hold the power button until the Apple logo displays to turn on the Apple Vision Pro.

**2. Sign in with your Apple ID:** During the initial setup, use the Apple Pencil or the on-screen keyboard to input your Apple ID and password.

**3. Turn on iCloud:** During the first setup procedure, make sure you turn on iCloud by following the prompts on the screen.

**4. Verify your iCloud settings:** To view your iCloud settings, choose Settings > Your Name > iCloud.

**5.** The Apple Vision Pro enables you to **access your iCloud data once activated**. You can see your iCloud Drive-stored documents, notes, and photographs, for instance.

**6. Manage iCloud Storage:** Select Settings > Your Name > iCloud > Manage Storage.

**7. Back up your Apple Vision Pro:** Select Settings > Your Name > iCloud > iCloud Backup to perform an iCloud backup of your Apple Vision Pro.

You can utilize iCloud on the Apple Vision Pro and have a flawless digital experience by following these instructions.

**Note:** You may use the Apple Support website to find troubleshooting methods if you run into any problems while utilizing iCloud on the Apple Vision Pro.

# Setting a passcode and using Optic ID

To protect your device and ensure easy, safe access, you must set a PIN and use Optic ID on the Apple Vision Pro. Using Optic ID and setting a password are explained in detail in the following guide:

## Setting a Password:

**1.** To enable password protection, go to Settings > Password on your Apple Vision Pro.

**2.** In case it isn't activated already, tap "Turn Passcode On.".

**3.** To ensure it works, type in a six-digit passcode twice.

**4.** Alternatively, by selecting "Passcode Options," you can use a four-digit numeric code or a unique alphanumeric code.

**5.** After you set the passcode, you can adjust other parameters, like whether Face ID or Touch ID is necessary and how long it will take until the password is needed.

## Using Optic ID:

**1.** To securely unlock your Apple Vision Pro and confirm access to sensitive data, utilize Optic ID, a state-of-the-art biometric authentication tool that leverages cutting-edge face recognition technology.

**2.** To configure Optic ID, choose Settings > Optic ID.

**3.** To enroll your face, follow the on-screen directions. In order to get various facial angles, you usually move your head in a circular manner.

**4.** After enrollment, Optic ID is ready to be used to authorize secure activities and unlock your device.

You may secure your Apple Vision Pro and take advantage of the smooth biometric authentication process by setting a password and using Optic ID, as shown in these instructions.

## Connecting Bluetooth accessories

Use the following procedures to connect Bluetooth devices to the Apple Vision Pro:

**1.** To **turn on Apple Vision Pro**, press and hold the power button until the Apple logo displays to turn on the Apple Vision Pro.

**2. Go to Settings**. Press the gear symbol to launch the Settings app by sliding down from the top of the screen.

**3. Go to Settings** > Bluetooth and choose Bluetooth.

**4. Enable Bluetooth:** If Bluetooth isn't already enabled, press the Bluetooth switch.

**5. Pair your item:** Set your Bluetooth accessory to pairing mode and watch for it to show up on your Apple Vision Pro's device list. To match an item, tap its name.

**6. Enter a passcode (if required):** Use the Apple Pencil or the on-screen keyboard to enter the password if your accessory needs one.

**7. Check connection:** After connecting, go to Settings > Bluetooth to examine your Bluetooth connection. If your Bluetooth device has a checkbox next to it, you are linked.

You may have a flawless digital experience by connecting Bluetooth items to the Apple Vision Pro and following these instructions.

**Note:** You may find troubleshooting instructions on the Apple Support page if you have any problems connecting Bluetooth items to the Apple Vision Pro.

## Using AirDrop

With the Apple Vision Pro, you can easily share images, movies, documents, and more with other Apple devices by using AirDrop. This is a thorough tutorial on using AirDrop.

**1. Turn on Wi-Fi and Bluetooth.** In order to utilize AirDrop, make sure that both of these features are on. To do this, swipe down from the top of the screen to reveal Control Center, then press the icons for Bluetooth and Wi-Fi.

**2. Access the Content to Exchange:** Open the image, movie, or file that you wish to exchange. For instance, to share a picture, use the Photos app.

**3. View the Share Menu:** To access the Share menu, press and hold the content or tap the "Share" icon inside the app.

**4. Select AirDrop from the Share menu.** Press it to continue.

**5. Select the recipient:** With your Apple Vision Pro, an AirDrop-enabled device search will start for all nearby devices. You may then touch the device you want to share with them after it has located them.

**6. An alert will be sent to the receiver** requesting that they accept the AirDrop. Once they agree to the transfer, the system will download the material to their device.

**7. Verify the Status of the Transfer:** You will receive a notification once the transfer is complete.

You can improve the Apple Vision Pro's smooth and integrated experience by using these methods to swiftly and wirelessly exchange material with other Apple devices using AirDrop.

## Using Family Sharing

You may share purchases, subscriptions, and other material with up to six family members on the Apple Vision Pro by using family sharing. This is a thorough tutorial on how to utilize family sharing:

**1. To begin configuring Family Sharing,** select Settings > Your Name > Family Sharing. To create your family group and extend an invitation to family members to join, follow the steps on the screen.

**2. Share Purchases:** After setting up Family Sharing, you can share purchases you make with your family on the App Store, Apple Music, Apple TV+, and other Apple services. To distribute an order, go to the order page and choose "Share with Family."

**3. Split Subscriptions:** Another option is to split subscriptions among family members. Go to Settings > Your Name > Subscriptions, choose the subscription you want to share, and then click OK. If you would like to share the subscription with any family members, tap "Share with Family" and choose them.

**4. Share iCloud Storage:** Go to Settings > Your Name > Family Sharing > iCloud Storage. Choose "Share with Family" to share the desired storage capacity.

**5. Set Up Screen Time:** Go to Settings > Screen Time > Family to configure screen time for your family members. This allows you to restrict your family members' use of apps, access to content, and amount of screen time.

**6. Share Location:** Go to Settings > Your Name > Family Sharing > Share My Location to allow family members to see where you are. By using the Find My Family app, you may also see where your family members are located.

By following these instructions, you can improve the smooth and integrated experience of Apple Vision Pro by using Family Sharing to share purchases, subscriptions, and other material with your family members.

# Chapter 4. Product Installation Guide

## How to install Apple Vision Pro

Unpacking, adjusting the fit, and turning on the device are the simple steps involved in installing the Apple Vision Pro. This is a thorough installation instruction for the Apple Vision Pro:

**1. Carefully take the Apple Vision Pro** out of its packaging and make sure all of the parts are inside, such as the power adapter, charging cord, and headset.

**2. The Apple Vision Pro has dials and straps** that you can adjust to guarantee a snug and comfortable fit. To fine-tune the fit and adjust the straps to suit your head, use the dial.

**3. Turn on the headset** by pressing and holding the power button until the Apple logo displays. To finish the initial setup, connect to Wi-Fi and sign in with your Apple ID by following the on-screen prompts.

**4. Customize and Secure:** Utilize the Apple Vision Pro's built-in privacy and security features to safeguard your Apple ID, as well as display settings and work-related configurations.

**5. Make sure your Apple Vision Pro is running the most current software update.** To check if any updates are available, go to Settings > General > Software Update.

Follow these instructions to install the Apple Vision Pro and have a flawless digital experience.

**Note:** You may find troubleshooting instructions on the Apple Support page if you run into any problems installing the Apple Vision Pro.

## Adjusting the fit of Apple Vision Pro

Adjusting the fit of the Apple Vision Pro is crucial for the best possible augmented reality experience. This is a thorough tutorial that explains how to modify the Apple Vision Pro's fit:

**1. Carefully take the Apple Vision Pro** out of its packaging and make sure all of the parts are inside, such as the power adapter, charging cord, and headset.

**2. Put on the Apple Vision Pro:** After adjusting the straps to suit your head, place the device on your head. Not too tight, but just snug enough, are the straps.

**3. Dial Adjustment:** To fine-tune the fit, use the dial on the headset's rear. To adjust the fit, turn the dial counterclockwise to loosen it and clockwise to tighten it.

**4. Modify the Nose Pad:** Ensure a comfortable fit by adjusting the nose pad. To change the nose pad's position, gently press it up or down.

**5. Modify the Interpupillary Distance** to ensure your lenses are positioned correctly. To change the IPD, use the slider on the headset's bottom.

**6. Verify the Fit:** After making any adjustments, make sure the Apple Vision Pro is snug and comfortable. The headset shouldn't slip down your face or move around.

By following these instructions, you can customize the Apple Vision Pro's fit for a safe and comfortable augmented reality experience.

# Attaching or removing the Apple Vision Pro Light Seal

Use the methods below to connect or remove the Light Seal from the Apple Vision Pro:

## Putting the light seal on:

**1.** Make sure the Apple Vision Pro is resting on a sturdy surface, such as a desk or table.

**2.** Place the Light Seal Cushion facing outward, so that it contacts your face when you put it on, and line it up with the frame.

**3.** The light seal and the frame should feel magnetically connected.

## Removing the light seal:

**1.** Pull the light seal gently until it separates from the frame in order to remove it.

Use these procedures to put the Light Seal Cushion on or take it off:

## The Light Seal Cushion Attachment:

**1.** Position the Light Seal Cushion so that it contacts your face when you put it on, aligning it with the Light Seal.

**2.** The light seal cushion and light seal should feel magnetically connected.

## Removing the light seal cushion:

**1.** Pull the light seal cushion gently until it separates from the light seal in order to remove it.

For a safe and enjoyable experience, it's essential to apply the appropriate size of Light Seal and Light Seal Cushion to your face. When using the Apple Vision Pro, use the Light Seal and Light Seal Cushion at all times; never wear the gadget unattached. This improves comfort and lessens the possibility of facial and eye injuries.

You may also like to use the detachable solo knit band or dual loop band, which can be adjusted to provide a precise and comfortable fit, for a more customized fit.

You can either put the Light Seal and Light Seal Cushion on the Apple Vision Pro or remove them by following these steps.

# Chapter 5. Setup and Configuration

## Adjusting settings on Apple Vision Pro

Changing the Apple Vision Pro's settings is crucial to guaranteeing peak performance and personalizing your experience. This is a thorough tutorial that explains how to change the Apple Vision Pro's settings:

**1. Access Settings:** To open the Control Center and hit the gear symbol, scroll down from the top of the screen to see the settings.

**2. Display Settings:** You can adjust the display's brightness, contrast, and color temperature here. Additionally, you have the option to activate or deactivate True Tone, which modifies the display's color temperature in response to outside light.

**3. Audio Settings:** Under the Audio settings, you can change the spatial audio on/off and alter the level.

**4. Privacy Settings:** You may control which applications and services have access to your location, camera, microphone, and other private information by going to the Privacy Settings.

**5. Accessibility options:** To improve the device's usability for those with impairments, you may activate features like VoiceOver, Zoom, and Magnifier under the Accessibility options.

**6. General Settings:** Manage Wi-Fi, Bluetooth, cellular, and VPN settings in the General settings. In addition, you have the ability to control software upgrades, screen time, and your Apple ID.

**7. Optic ID Settings:** Here, you can adjust facial recognition settings, such as turning on or off Optic ID, configuring a different look, and controlling Optic ID settings specific to a certain app.

**8. Passcode Settings:** Here, you can control passcode-related settings, including activating and disabling passcodes, configuring Touch ID or Face ID, and adjusting passcode requirements.

You may tweak the Apple Vision Pro's settings and personalize your experience to your liking by following these instructions.

## Using Control Center

Quick access to important settings and functionality is possible with the Apple Vision Pro by using the Control Center. Here is a thorough how-to manual for Control Center:

**1. Control Center Access:** To open the Control Center, swipe down from the upper-right corner of the screen. This will cause the Control Center to open, including a number of settings and controls.

**2. Functions of Control Center:**

*Connectivity:* With Control Center, you can easily access and control functions including Bluetooth, Wi-Fi, cellular data, and airplane mode.

*Audio Controls:* You may change the audio output choices, activate or deactivate spatial audio, and modify the volume.

*Display Settings:* Brightness and True Tone are just two of the easy-to-access display settings available via Control Center.

***Optic ID and accessibility features:***
VoiceOver and Magnifier are accessible, and you may easily activate or disable Optic ID.

***Battery and Device Functions:*** You can access device functions like Power Off, Restart, and Lock Screen as well as check the battery level via the Control Center.

**3. Personalizing the Control Center:** You have the option to add more features and functions to the Control Center. To do this, go to Settings > Control Center and select "Customize Controls."You may now reorganize, add, and delete controls to best fit your requirements.

**4. Closing Control Center:** To exit the Control Center, touch anywhere outside of it or swipe up from the bottom of the screen.

The Apple Vision Pro's usefulness and convenience are increased by utilizing the

Control Center, which gives you quick and easy access to a variety of settings and options.

## Managing two-factor authentication for your Apple ID

Two-factor authentication provides crucial security for your Apple ID. This is a thorough tutorial that will help you manage your Apple ID's two-factor authentication:

**1. Turn on two-factor authentication:** To turn on two-factor authentication, navigate to Settings > Your Name > Password & Security > Two-Factor Authentication. To set your Apple ID up for two-factor authentication, follow the on-screen instructions.

**2. Make Use of Two-Factor Authentication:** Whenever you sign in to your Apple ID on a new device or browser, once two-factor authentication is activated, you will be asked to input a verification code sent to your trusted device or phone number.

**3. Manage trusted devices:** To manage your trusted devices, go to Settings > Your Name > Password & Security > Trusted Devices. You may modify, delete, or add trusted devices from this page.

**4. Recovery Key:** If you are unable to access your trusted devices, Apple offers a recovery key that you may use to get back into your account. Navigate to Settings > Your Name > Password & Security > Recovery Key.

**5. Manage Trusted Phone Numbers:** To manage your trusted phone numbers, go to Settings > Your Name > Password & Security > Trusted Phone Numbers. You may change, delete, or add trusted phone numbers from here.

**6. Disable Two-Factor Authentication:**
To disable two-factor authentication, go to Settings > Your Name > Password & Security > Two-Factor Authentication. Disabling two-factor authentication, however, is not advised, as it makes your Apple ID less secure.

By following these instructions, you can secure your Apple Vision Pro's security and handle two-factor authentication for your Apple ID.

## Creating and managing Hide My Email addresses

When using the Apple Vision Pro, creating and maintaining Hide My Email addresses is a helpful tool that helps keep your privacy safe. You can find a comprehensive guide on setting up and maintaining Hide My Email addresses here:

**1. To access Hide My Email:** Go to Settings > Your Name > iCloud > Hide My Email.

**2. Create a Hide My Email Address:** Click "Create New Email Address" to start the process of creating a Hide My Email address. To forward emails to your main email address, you must first create a unique email address.

**3. Modify Your Hide My Email Addresses:** Navigate to Settings > Your Name > iCloud > Hide My Email. You have the ability to see, modify, or remove Hide My Email addresses from this page.

**4. Edit a hidden email address:** To make changes to the address you want to change, simply tap on it. You have the option to remove the Hide My Email address or modify the forwarding email address.

**5. Eliminate a hidden Here's my email address:** To do so, tap on the Hide My Email address you want to remove. To ensure the deletion is complete, tap "Delete Email Address.".

**6. Share a Hide My Email address:** Tap on the address you want to share in order to share a Hide My Email address. When registering for a service or creating an account, tap "Copy" to copy the Hide My Email address to your clipboard, then paste it into the relevant area.

You can protect your privacy while using the Apple Vision Pro by creating and managing Hide My Email addresses and following these procedures.

## Protecting your web browsing with iCloud Private Relay

iCloud Private Relay is a powerful feature that enhances your security and privacy while using the internet on the Apple Vision Pro for online surfing protection. This guide provides a detailed explanation on how to maximize the benefits of iCloud Private Relay:

**1. Using iCloud Private Relay:** To access the iCloud Private Relay, navigate to Settings > [Your Name] > iCloud > Private Relay.

**2. Activating iCloud Private Relay:** To activate iCloud Private Relay, press the toggle. When turned on, your device will encrypt the website you are viewing and mask your IP address by passing it via two different internet relays.

**3. iCloud Private Relay's Function:** This feature makes sure that no one organization, not even Apple, is able to determine your identity or the websites you visit. Apple owns one part of your IP address, while a third-party network provider owns the other.

**4. Setting Up: There are two options available:** "Maintain General Location" and

"Use Country and Time Zone." While the second option gives websites your country and time zone, the first option helps prevent websites from pinpointing your exact location.

**5. iCloud Private Relay Benefits:** When you use iCloud Private Relay, you get an extra level of protection and privacy when browsing the internet. It shields your IP address from exploitation to create a profile about you and prevents third parties from monitoring your location and online activities.

**6. Restrictions:** Although iCloud Private Relay is an effective tool for safeguarding your online activities, it's important to remember that not all users or locations may have access to it. It could also not function with every network or internet service provider.

These instructions will help you secure your online surfing using iCloud Private Relay, improving your privacy and security while using the Apple Vision Pro to browse the internet.

## Using a private network address

When using the Apple Vision Pro to browse the internet, one helpful feature that improves security and privacy is the use of a private network address. This is a thorough tutorial on using a private network address.

**1. Finding the Private Network Address:** Select Settings > Wi-Fi to get to the private network address.

**2. Activating a Private Network Address:** To activate a Private Network Address, flip the switch. When enabled, your device will make it more difficult for other parties to trace you by using a new MAC address for every Wi-Fi network you connect to.

**3. How Private Network Address Works:**
Rather than utilizing the specific MAC address
of your device, Private Network Address
creates a random MAC address for every Wi-Fi
network you connect to. This lessens the
possibility that someone else may follow your
device and internet activities.

**4. Advantages of a Private Network
Address:** When using Wi-Fi networks, a
private network address adds an extra degree
of protection and privacy. It safeguards your
MAC address to prevent the creation of a
profile about you and to deter third parties
from monitoring your device and internet
activities.

**5. Restrictions:** Although a private network
address is an effective tool for securing your
privacy and security, it's vital to remember that
not all people or all areas may have access to it.
Furthermore, it may not function with all
routers or Wi-Fi networks.

You may utilize a private network address to improve security and privacy while using Wi-Fi networks on the Apple Vision Pro by following these instructions.

# Chapter 6. Use Cases

## Examples of how to use Apple Vision Pro

I've compiled a list of several use cases that highlight the Apple Vision Pro's adaptability and potential in order to provide a thorough and engaging explanation of how to use it.

**1. Immersive Gaming:** With its motion controllers, spatial audio, and high-resolution screens, the Apple Vision Pro provides an immersive gaming experience. You may have a very immersive gaming experience by playing a variety of games, such as adventure and first-person shooters.

**2. Virtual Meetings:** With Apple Vision Pro, you can participate in highly interactive and immersive virtual meetings. The ability to view and communicate with other participants in a realistic way makes virtual meetings seem more like face-to-face conversations.

**3. Architecture and Design:** With the Apple Vision Pro, architects and designers can imagine and work with their ideas in a more natural and engaging manner. They may investigate their concepts from many viewpoints and angles, which improves the effectiveness and efficiency of the design process.

**4. Education:** A variety of educational environments, including classrooms, labs, and museums, may make use of the Apple Vision Pro. Allowing students to experience 3D models, simulations, and virtual worlds can make learning more dynamic and engaging.

**5. Training and Simulation:** A variety of sectors, including healthcare, aviation, and manufacturing, may benefit from the use of the Apple Vision Pro for training and simulation. It improves the effectiveness and efficiency of the training process by enabling students to experiment and learn in a secure setting.

**6. Entertainment:** Watching sports, movies, and TV programs are just a few of the entertainment options available with the Apple Vision Pro. With motion controllers, spatial audio, and high-resolution screens, you can have a completely immersive experience.

**7. Art and Creativity:** Painting, sculpting, and animation are just a few of the artistic and creative tasks that the Apple Vision Pro can do. It enables more intuitive and deep creative exploration for artists.

**8. Tourism and Travel:** You may utilize the Apple Vision Pro for tourism and travel activities, including making vacation plans, taking virtual tours, and exploring virtual locations. It is possible to go to other places in a more immersive and interactive manner, which enhances the fun and engagement of the trip.

By investigating these use cases, you can unlock the Apple Vision Pro's full potential and come up with creative new ways to utilize it in everyday life.

# Tips and tricks for getting the most out of Apple Vision Pro

Here are some pointers and suggestions to help you maximize the potential of the Apple Vision Pro:

**1. Customize the Control Center:** By customizing the Control Center, you can add more controls and commonly used features. In order to do this, go to Settings > Control Center and choose "Customize Controls." You may then reorganize the controls to better fit your requirements by adding, removing, or changing them.

**2. Make use of Siri:** With the Apple Vision Pro, Siri can assist you with a number of things, like making phone calls, sending messages, and setting reminders. To bring up Siri, say "Hey Siri" or press and hold the side button.

**3. Use Shortcuts:** With the Apple Vision Pro, shortcuts allow you to automate chores and create unique workflows. You may choose shortcuts for a number of functions, such as messaging, playing music, and obtaining directions. Go to the Shortcuts app and press the "+" icon to create a shortcut.

**4. Take advantage of Split View:** With the Apple Vision Pro, Split View lets you run two programs simultaneously. Drag an app to the left or right side of the screen to enable Split View. To access the dock, swipe up from the bottom of the screen.

**5. Use Picture in Picture:** With the Apple Vision Pro, you can use other applications to view movies or make FaceTime calls at the same time. To access the Home screen, swipe up from the bottom of the screen, and then hit the Picture in Picture button while in a chat or video to enable Picture in Picture.

**6. Make use of AirPlay:** This feature lets you transmit music and video from your Apple Vision Pro to other gadgets, such as HomePods or Apple TVs. To activate AirPlay, open the Control Center by swiping down from the top-right corner of the screen, then hit the AirPlay button.

**7. Use an Apple Pencil:** On the Apple Vision Pro, you can annotate documents, draw on them, and take notes using an Apple Pencil. To begin writing or drawing with the Apple Pencil, just touch the screen.

You may improve your experience and get the most out of the Apple Vision Pro by paying attention to these pointers and techniques.

# Chapter 7.
# Troubleshooting

## Common issues and how to solve them

There may be common problems with the Apple Vision Pro, and knowing how to solve them is crucial. This is a thorough reference on typical problems and their solutions:

### 1. Connectivity Issues:

- Try rebooting your device, the router, and the Bluetooth accessory if you're having trouble connecting to Wi-Fi or Bluetooth.

- Verify that the most recent software update is installed on your device.

- Reset your network settings by selecting Settings > General > Reset > Reset Network Settings if the problem still exists.

## 2. Depleting the battery immediately:

- Look for any background-running applications and end them if they are not in use.

- To maximize the battery's lifespan, adjust the display settings. Power-saving measures include turning down the brightness and turning on the auto-lock function.

- Try calibrating the batteries by completely charging and then discharging the device if the problem continues.

## 3. Performance issues:

- Make sure your device has enough storage space available if you see a drop in performance. To make space, you may remove any unnecessary media or programs.

- To free up memory and end any background programs that could be interfering with performance, restart your device.

## 4. App-Specific Issues:

- Make sure the app is updated to the most recent version if you have problems with a particular app.

- To fix any possible software bugs, consider uninstalling and reinstalling the program if the problem continues.

## 5. Display Issues:

- Try restarting your device to see if it fixes any display-related problems, such as flickering or unresponsiveness.

- If the problem continues, you may want to try tweaking the display settings or reaching out to Apple Support for further help.

**6. Audio Troubleshooting:**

- Make sure the device is not in quiet mode and that the volume is cranked up if you are having audio issues.

- Examine the speaker or microphone holes for any dirt or blockages, and clean them carefully if needed.

**7. Optic ID Troubleshooting:**

- Make sure the TrueDepth camera is clear of debris and clean if you have problems with Optic ID.

- Try re-enrolling your face in the Face ID settings if the problem continues.

### 8. General Troubleshooting:

- As a last option, if problems continue, think about doing a factory reset. Before you do this, make sure you have a backup of your data.

By following these troubleshooting instructions, you can effectively resolve typical difficulties that may arise with the Apple Vision Pro.

## Contacting Apple Support for further assistance

One simple and efficient way to resolve any issues with your Apple Vision Pro is to contact Apple Support. This is a thorough tutorial on how to get in touch with Apple Support if you need help:

**1. Go to the Apple Support website:** Visit the Apple Support website (https://support.apple.com/) to get information about the problem you are having. You may find a lot of useful information and troubleshooting procedures on the website to assist you in solving your issue.

**2. Use the Apple Support app:** To access support materials, arrange a conversation with an Apple help advisor, and monitor the progress of your help request, download the Apple Support app from the App Store.

**3. Make a phone call to Apple Support:** To talk with a support representative, call 1-800-MY-APPLE (1-800-692-7753). Make sure you have your Apple ID, device serial number, and a thorough description of the problem you are having on hand.

**4. Chat with Apple Support:** Go to the Apple Support website and select the "Chat" option to start a chat session with a support adviser. Make sure you have your Apple ID, device serial number, and a thorough description of the problem you are having on hand.

**5. Visit an Apple Store or Authorized Service Provider:** If online assistance isn't able to help you with your problem, you may want to check out an Apple Store or Authorized Service Provider. You contact 1-800-MY-APPLE or by visiting the Apple Support website, you may make an appointment to visit an Apple Store.

**6. Get ready for your support session:** In order to speed up the support process, collect the following data prior to calling Apple Support:
- Your Apple ID and device serial number
- A thorough explanation of the problem you're having
- Any error messages or codes you've come across
- Any previous troubleshooting attempts you've made

By following these instructions, you can effectively contact Apple Support for assistance with your Apple Vision Pro.

# Chapter 8. Frequently Asked Questions (FAQs)

## Answers to common questions about Apple Vision Pro

I've put together a list of commonly asked questions and their responses in order to offer a thorough and convincing guide to answers to frequently asked questions concerning the Apple Vision Pro.

First of all, what is the Apple Vision Pro?
Combining virtual reality (VR) and augmented reality (AR) technologies, the Apple Vision Pro is a mixed-reality headset that offers an engaging and interactive experience.

What distinguishing qualities does the Apple Vision Pro offer?

The Apple Vision Pro has motion controllers, spatial audio, high-resolution displays, and Optic ID facial recognition technology.

How much does the Apple Vision Pro cost?
Apple has not yet made the price of the Vision Pro public. However, it is expected to be a high-end product like other expensive AR/VR headsets.

When is the Apple Vision Pro going to be available?
The Apple Vision Pro's official release date is still unknown. However, it will be released earlier than expected.

The Apple Vision Pro runs on which operating system?
The Apple Vision Pro utilizes the latest version of iOS, designed specifically for mixed reality experiences.

Does the Apple Vision Pro need a console or another separate computer?

The Apple Vision Pro does not require a separate computer or console for use. It is a stand-alone gadget that uses an iPad or iPhone connection for configuration and content delivery.

Is it possible to play games with the Apple Vision Pro?

The Apple Vision Pro allows playing games. With motion controllers, spatial audio, and high-resolution displays, it provides an immersive and interactive experience.

Is it possible to use the Apple Vision Pro for productivity and work?

Yes, productivity and work usage are possible with the Apple Vision Pro. It provides a wide range of tools and applications for architecture, education, design, and other fields.

Does the Apple Vision Pro support wireless connectivity?
The Apple Vision Pro supports Bluetooth and Wi-Fi wireless connectivity.

Does the Apple Vision Pro support 5G connectivity?
The Apple Vision Pro does not support 5G connectivity. It does, however, support Bluetooth 5 and Wi-Fi 6.

Does the Apple Vision Pro support multiplayer gaming?
The Apple Vision Pro does indeed allow for multiplayer gaming. Through a range of games and experiences, it enables users to interact with and play with other users.

Is cross-platform gaming supported by the Apple Vision Pro?
The Apple Vision Pro supports cross-platform gaming with other Apple devices, such as the iPhone and iPad. Nevertheless, it is not

compatible with cross-platform gaming on other systems, like PCs or Android.

Yes, the Apple Vision Pro supports external displays.
The Apple Vision Pro does not support external displays. It does, however, allow content mirroring to other Apple devices, including the iPad and iPhone.

Can the Apple Vision Pro capture 360-degree images and videos?
The Apple Vision Pro can capture and process 360-degree images and videos. With its spatial audio and high-resolution displays, it provides an immersive and interactive experience.

Is 3D modeling and design supported by the Apple Vision Pro?
The Apple Vision Pro supports 3D modeling and design. It provides a wide range of tools and applications for architecture, design, and other fields.

You can learn more about the features and capabilities of Apple Vision Pro by answering some frequently asked questions. For further information and supplementary resources, please consult the Apple Vision Pro User Guide and the official Apple Support resources.

# Chapter 9. Product Description Content

## Detailed description of Apple Vision Pro

Combining virtual reality (VR) and augmented reality (AR) technology, the Apple Vision Pro is a mixed reality headset that offers an engaging and interactive experience. With its seamless integration of digital material and the real environment, it is Apple's first spatial computer, enabling users to maintain a sense of presence and interpersonal connection. This is a thorough explanation of the Apple Vision Pro:

**Design and Features:**

- The Apple Vision Pro is made out of a single piece of laminated glass that has been three-dimensionally created. It flows into an aluminum alloy frame, which bends to encircle the user's face.

- The Light Seal provides a perfect fit while obstructing stray light by softly flexing to suit the user's face.

- The Apple Vision Pro can be precisely adjusted to the user's head with the Fit Dial, and the Solo Knit Band offers cushioning, breathability, and elasticity.

- For a more customized fit, the Dual Loop Band provides an extra choice.

- The Apple Vision Pro has motion controllers, spatial audio, high-resolution displays, and Optic ID face recognition technology.

- The gadget runs the most recent version of iOS, which was created with mixed reality experiences in mind.

- For setup and content delivery, it is a stand-alone gadget that connects to the user's iPhone or iPad.

- Both Bluetooth and Wi-Fi wireless communication are supported by the Apple Vision Pro.

## Display and Audio:

- The Apple Vision Pro has two screens with ultra-high-definition display technology that packs 23 million pixels to provide breathtaking colors and detail.

- More pixels are sent to each eye by the specialized micro-OLED display technology than by a 4K TV.

- The sophisticated spatial audio technology adapts the sound to the area and produces the illusion that noises are emanating from the user's surroundings.

- Personalized spatial audio is delivered by two independently amplified drivers within each audio pod, which are matched to the user's head and ear shapes.

**Eye tracking and optical ID:**

- The Apple Vision Pro's high-speed cameras and ring of LEDs display user-friendly input as part of its high-performance eye tracking technology.

- A new identification mechanism called Optic ID uses an iris analysis to open Vision Pro, autofill passwords, and finish Apple Pay transactions.

- Another feature of EyeSight is a visual signal that lets others know when a user is taking a spatial picture or video.

## Spatial Computing:

- With the Apple Vision Pro, users may navigate with only their hands, eyes, and voices by seamlessly fusing digital material with the real environment.

- Digital material may be interacted with by users in a manner that makes it seem as if it is really there in their environment.

- With the Apple Vision Pro, programs may run on an endless canvas that extends beyond the confines of a conventional display.

- With the help of the gadget, users may organize applications in any location and resize them to the ideal size, realizing their fantasy workplace.

- With the Apple Vision Pro, you can turn any space into a personal theater where you can enjoy games, movies, and TV programs at the ideal size and experience being a part of the action thanks to Spatial Audio.

- Numerous tools and apps for design, architecture, teaching, and other fields are available on the tablet.

**Privacy and Security:**

- Apple Vision Pro provides the best privacy and security in business.

- No information pertaining to eye tracking is sent to Apple, outside applications, or websites.

- When a user is using an app or is completely absorbed in an activity, EyeSight makes their eyes visible and notifies people in close proximity.

- Apple Vision Pro simultaneously shows the user's eyes to the person approaching and allows the user to see them.

The innovative Apple Vision Pro provides an immersive and engaging experience. It creates new avenues for work, play, and self-expression with its cutting edge technology and smooth interaction with the real world.

## Technical specifications and requirements

I've put up a list of essential features and specs for the Apple Vision Pro in order to provide a thorough and appealing reference on its technical specifications and needs.

**Display:**

- Two bespoke micro-OLED screens with a 23 million pixel resolution overall

- 50% brighter than the iPhone 12 Pro Max

- 1000 nits of average brightness and 1200 nits of peak brightness - 1152 x 1444 pixels per eye

- 90 Hz refresh rate

- P3 broad color spectrum

- Contrast ratio of 20:1

**Audio features include:**

- Personalized spatial audio depending on the user's head and ear shape

- The high-performance eye tracking system includes ultra-fast cameras and an LED ring.

- Spatial audio with two separately amplified speakers per audio pod

**Motion controllers:**

- two action buttons,

- two touch surfaces,

- haptic feedback,

- six degrees of freedom (6DoF) motion tracking

**Sensors:**

- Face ID camera;

- proximity sensor;

- ambient light sensor;

- three-axis accelerometer;

- three-axis magnetometer;

- six-axis gyroscope

**Connectivity:**

- Wi-Fi 6 (802.11ax)

- Bluetooth 5.0

- USB-C connector for connectivity

**Battery and power**

- lithium-ion rechargeable battery

- maximum use of three hours on a single charge

- Connector for magnetic charging

**Headset measurements are as follows:**

- 19.2 cm (7.56 inches) in width, 18.2 cm (7.09 inches) in height, and 10.5 cm (4.14 inches) in depth.

- Motion controllers: 6.5 inches long, 3.8 inches broad, and 10.8 inches (4.25 inches deep) in diameter.

- Weight: 398 grams (14.1 ounces) for the headset, 134 grams (4.7 ounces each) for the motion controllers.

**Operating System:**

- iOS 16 is the operating system (created especially for mixed reality experiences).

**System requirements include:**

- Bluetooth 5.0 or later,

- Wi-Fi 6 (802.11ax) or later,

- iPad running iOS 16, iPhone, or later.

You will be able to learn more about the Apple Vision Pro and its capabilities by providing these technical specs and prerequisites.

# Chapter 10. Potential Product Risks and How to Solve Them

## Risks associated with using Apple Vision Pro

Although the Apple Vision Pro provides an innovative experience in spatial computing, there are various hazards and privacy and security-related issues to be aware of. Potential data collection, privacy concerns, and security flaws are some of these issues. Numerous sensors, cameras, and microphones on the gadget may pose a security and privacy issue if they are hacked. Additionally, advertising, data brokers, or even government agencies may find interest in the device's vast amount of recorded data. As with any linked device, there's also the risk of unwanted access and subsequent exploitation by hackers.

To address these issues, Apple has put in place a number of privacy and security measures to protect user data. These include precautions to prevent eye tracking data from being shared with Apple, third-party applications, or websites; protections to limit the data the device collects; and indications to alert users when the device is recording. The business has also unveiled EyeSight, an external display that indicates when the device is in use, and Optic ID, an authentication solution that leverages the uniqueness of a user's iris for secure authentication.

Consumers should exercise caution and carefully evaluate the privacy implications before using the Apple Vision Pro, despite Apple's active efforts to mitigate these concerns. Users should read the privacy statement, use the device sensibly and carefully, and stay updated on security and privacy upgrades. As with any new technology, it's critical to exercise caution and understand any possible privacy and security risks before using it.

In conclusion, while the Apple Vision Pro provides a revolutionary experience in spatial computing, users should be aware of the possible privacy and security threats. Users may enjoy the gadget's unique features and make educated choices about how to use it while safeguarding their security and privacy by being aware of these dangers and taking the necessary precautions.

## How to mitigate risks and ensure safe use

Utilize the following best practices and advice to ensure responsible and safe use of the Apple Vision Pro while reducing any potential risks:

**1. Read the privacy policy** to understand how your data is gathered, processed, and shared before using the Apple Vision Pro. This will enable you to use the equipment with knowledge while making selections.

**2. Take advantage of Optic ID:** This safe authentication method leverages your iris' distinctiveness to provide secure identification. For password autofill and device unlocking, use Optic ID; stay away from alternative authentication techniques that can jeopardize your privacy.

**3. Be mindful of eye sight.** Eye sight is a visual cue that lets others know when you are taking pictures or movies in three dimensions. Be mindful of EyeSight's activation and avoid using it in private or sensitive settings.

**4. Limit data collection:** To enhance the user experience and provide tailored information, Apple Vision Pro gathers data. By changing the device's settings, you can restrict the amount of data gathered. For example, you can disable the eye tracking function when it is not required or deactivate location services.

**5. Maintain your device's updates:** Update your Apple Vision Pro on a regular basis to make sure you have the most recent privacy and security features. Updates may enhance your device's overall performance and shield it against known vulnerabilities.

**6. Use strong passwords:** For your Apple ID and any other accounts connected to the Apple Vision Pro, use secure, one-of-a-kind passwords. Don't use information that can be guessed, such as your name, birthday, or everyday terms.

**7. Turn on two-factor authentication:** To increase your Apple ID's security, turn on two-factor authentication. This will help protect your account from unwanted access even if your password is hacked.

**8. Exercise caution while using third-party applications:** Since these apps could have access to your data, exercise caution when using them. Download software only from reputable stores, such as the App Store, and ensure that you read the privacy statement before using the program.

**9. Be aware of your surroundings:** When using the Apple Vision Pro, pay attention to your surroundings, particularly in public areas. Steer clear of using the gadget on crowded trains, public restrooms, or other places where privacy is an issue.

**10. Contact Apple Support** immediately if you suspect your data has been exploited or your Apple Vision Pro has been hacked. This will help Apple look into the matter and take the necessary steps to protect your security and privacy.

Adhere to these best practices and advice to ensure the safe and responsible use of the Apple Vision Pro. You may consult the Apple Vision Pro User Guide and the official Apple Support pages for more information and supplementary resources.

Please consider leaving a 5-star review if you found the tutorial to be useful so that others may also learn about the new Apple Vision Pro.